Strings in Step

violin

BOOK
ONE

Jan Dobbins

Music Department
OXFORD UNIVERSITY PRESS
Oxford and New York

TEACHERS' NOTES

This book introduces pupils to the basics of string playing. Information is presented in a logical order and reinforced at each stage. The series is suitable for group or individual tuition.

Technique, care of the instrument, note reading, sight-reading, intonation, improvisation, and composition are introduced and consolidated through the use of diagrams, games, and worksheets. Pupils enjoy colouring the diagrams and reading the comments of the cartoon characters.

Pupils' progress

An average rate of progress for 7–9-year-olds would be the completion of each section in ten to twelve weeks. Although new information is introduced throughout the book the material does not become any more difficult to play after the traditional tunes on pages 41 and 42. This encourages children to move on to the end of the book with a feeling of success and gives time for the establishment of a good technique before moving on to Book 2.

Pupils are encouraged to take an interest in their own progress by keeping a record of weekly practice and by planning their own concert performances. The achievement record, to be filled in by the teacher, indicates progress to parents and children, while increasing the pupils' feelings of success and generating enthusiasm to continue.

How to use the book

1. Keep left hand fingerwork and bowing separate until both are firmly established.
2. Use the bowing patterns often.
3. When introducing new tunes or exercises, ask pupils to listen to, then sing and clap each exercise before they play. The short exercises enable pupils to concentrate on technique and intonation as they play.
4. Revise past work thoroughly.
5. Use the colour coding system.
6. Give time to improvisation and composition using bowing and finger patterns as a starting-point.

Colour coding

To help pupils develop their understanding of which finger to use and where to place it, use the colour coding system and encourage pupils to colour in all the charts which show finger numbers, letter names, and notes. It is a good idea to supervise the colouring so that there are no mistakes. The colour coding system is developed in Book 2 to aid the understanding of finger patterns and their relationship to major and minor keys. When teaching large groups put dots of the correct colour on each diagram so that they can be coloured in at home.

First finger   – red
Second finger – yellow
Third finger   – green
Fourth finger – blue

Initially it is useful to put self-adhesive dots in the appropriate places on the fingerboard underneath the D string.

Theory worksheets

These may be completed an exercise at a time or a whole worksheet at one sitting.

2

Piano accompaniments P

All tunes and exercises which have piano accompaniments are marked with the letter 'p' in the Pupil Books. The page number for the Pupil Book is given at the top of each piece in the Piano Book. Accompaniments are provided for all tunes and exercises in Book 1 with the following exceptions:

a) Exercises which cannot be played in ensemble with all instruments, i.e. p. 22; p. 24, exx. 1–4; p. 31; p. 49, exx. 1–3.

b) The rounds, which are best unaccompanied.

The Open Strings Pizzicato (Pupil Book pages 10 and 11):

The accompaniments are lyrical and exciting enough for the pupils to feel that they are playing real pieces right from the start.

Later these pieces can be played with the bow.

Pizzicato Tunes on the D String (Pupil Book page 13):

Accompaniments are given for all the tunes in E, A, D, G, and C majors so that pupils can practise using the finger pattern on each string as they become familiar with the tunes.

A tune using the second finger is included for cellists only.

The tunes can be played using the bow as pupils become more proficient. Some of the tunes appear further on in the book in notated form. The familiarity of these tunes encourages note reading.

The fourth finger is introduced on page 13. Violin and viola pupils can be encouraged to play the 'Fourth Finger March' regularly as preparation for the introduction of the fourth finger in Section 3.

Bowing Patterns (Pupil Book page 19):

These can be introduced at the teacher's discretion. They are grouped together for convenience, but it is not necessary to cover them all at once.

When learning each of the major scales it is useful to play them using the bowing pattern rhythms. Examples of accompaniments for these are given in the keys of A, D, G, and C majors.

Ensemble playing

Encourage two-part ensemble playing from the start. Use hand clapping, knee slapping, and finger clicking for accompaniments to the tunes. Half the group play, the other half accompany with percussive rhythms.

Try 'I hear Thunder' (Pupil Book page 33) as a round as soon as pupils are familiar with the notes.

'Merry Dance' and 'Satellite Serenade' can be played as solos by the individual instruments or as three-part ensembles.

'Little Bird' has an easy second part to accommodate pupils in group lessons who progress at different rates and to provide an opportunity for duet work.

The cello book contains a second part for 'Moon Waltz' to introduce cello pupils to the idea of playing the bass line in an ensemble.

The rounds are a good way to introduce four-part ensemble playing. When all the strings play together interesting and effective performances can be produced by combining the instruments in various ways.

N.B. Tunes or exercises which cannot be played in ensemble with the other instruments in the series are indicated by an asterisk, ✱ .

Jan Dobbins 1991

CONTENTS

SECTION 1

SECTION 2

SECTION 3

The Violin

- scroll
- peg
- neck
- strings
- finger board
- sound holes
- bridge
- sound post
- fine tuners (adjusters)
- tail piece
- chin rest
- tail gut

The Bow

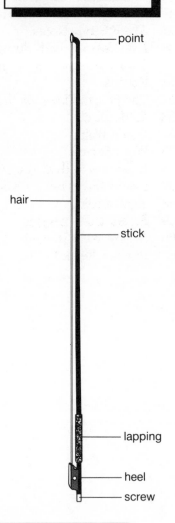

- point
- hair
- stick
- lapping
- heel
- screw

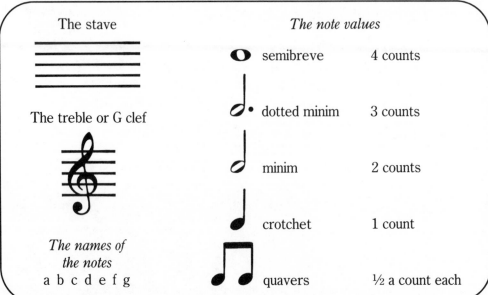

The stave

The treble or G clef

The names of the notes
a b c d e f g

The note values

𝅝	semibreve	4 counts
𝅗𝅥.	dotted minim	3 counts
𝅗𝅥	minim	2 counts
𝅘𝅥	crotchet	1 count
𝅘𝅥𝅮𝅘𝅥𝅮	quavers	½ a count each

Care of the Violin and Bow

1. Always put the violin away in the case after practice, wrapped in a cloth.

2. Never leave the violin in the sun or near a radiator.

3. Tighten the hair before you play.
   Loosen the hair before you put the bow away.

4. Remember to resin your bow.
   Never put anything but resin on your bow.

5. Avoid touching the bow hair with your fingers.

6. Leave a duster in your case to clean your violin and keep it free from resin.

Balancing the violin

The Violin

Name the parts of the violin:

Scroll	Peg
Neck	Fingerboard
Strings	Bridge
Sound hole	Sound post
Fine tuners	Tail piece
Tail gut	Chin rest

The Names of the Violin Strings

G   D   A   E

Ⓖ A B C Ⓓ E F G Ⓐ B C D Ⓔ F G A B

The Open Strings Pizzicato

'Pizzicato' means to pluck the string.

P ### The D string

Count:	1	2	3	4
	D	D	D	D
	D	D	D	D
	D	D	D	D
	D	D	D	D

P ### The A string

Count:	1	2	3	4
	A	A	A	A
	A	A	A	A
	A	A	A	A
	A	A	A	A

P ### The D and A strings

Count:	1	2	3	4
	D	D	D	D
	A	A	A	A
	D	D	D	D
	A	A	D	D

P

Pizzicato in Waltz Time

Count:	1	2	3	1	2	3
	A	A	A	A	A	A
	D	D	D	D	D	D
	A	A	A	A	A	A
	D	–	–	D	–	–

P*   **The E string**

Count:	1	2	3	4
	E	E	E	E
	E	E	E	E
	E	E	E	E
	E	E	E	E

P   **The G string**

Count:	1	2	3	4
	G	G	G	G
	G	G	G	G
	G	G	G	G
	G	G	G	G

P   **All four strings**

Count:	1	2	3	4
	G	G	G	G
	D	D	D	D
	A	A	A	A
	E	E	E	E

P

String Waltz

Count:	1	2	3	1	2	3
	E	E	E	A	A	A
	D	D	D	D	D	D
	G	G	G	D	D	D
	A	A	A	D	–	–

The Left Hand Finger Numbers

Pizzicato Tunes on the D String

P   *Hopscotch*

| 0 0 0 0 | 1 1 1 1 | 0 0 0 0 | 1 1 1 1 |
| 0 0 0 0 | 1 1 1 1 | 1 1 1 1 | 0 – 0 – |

P   *Hill Climbing*

| 0 0 0 0 | 1 1 1 1 | 2 2 2 2 | 3 3 3 3 |
| 2 2 2 2 | 1 1 1 1 | 0 0 0 0 | 0 – 0 – |

P   *Moonlight*

| 0 0 0 1 | 2 – 1 – | 0 2 1 1 | 0 – – – |
| 0 0 0 1 | 2 – 1 – | 0 2 1 1 | 0 – – – |

P   *Rainbows*

| 0 0 2 2 | 1 1 3 – | 0 0 2 2 | 1 1 1 – |
| 2 2 2 2 | 3 3 3 – | 3 3 2 2 | 1 1 0 – |

P   *Jumping Jack*

| 0 1 2 0 | 1 2 3 – | 2 2 2 2 | 1 1 1 – |
| 0 1 2 0 | 1 2 3 – | 2 2 1 1 | 0 0 0 – |

P   *Fourth Finger March*

| 0 1 2 3 | 4 4 4 4 | 4 3 2 1 | 0 – 0 – |

When you can play these tunes on the D string try them on the A, E or G string.

Concert Performance Idea

Choose a tune you can play really well and think of some words to fit the tune. Then try out this plan:

INTRODUCTION	Count 4 twice;
TUNE ON E	Pizzicato;
LINK	Count 4 twice;
TUNE ON A	Play pizzicato and sing the words;
LINK	Count 4 twice;
TUNE ON D	With the bow, or pizzicato with singing;
LINK	Count 4 twice;
TUNE ON G	Pizzicato.

The Bow

Name the parts of the bow:

Point
Hair
Heel
Screw
Lapping
Stick

14

The Bow Hold

Prepare the bow hold by making a circle with your thumb and middle finger:

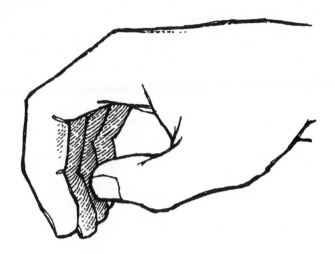

The thumb should be curved and flexible with the right corner of the thumbnail against the stick.

The second and third fingers rest lightly over the bow stick.

The little finger must stand on the stick and curve gently.

Imagine that your bow is a bird:
if you hold it too tightly you will kill it;
if you hold it too lightly
it will fly away.

Note Learning Game

Hold your hand out and pretend it is the stave. Your fingers are the lines of the stave. The spaces between your fingers are the spaces of the stave. Use these sentences to help you remember the names of the notes on the lines and in the spaces.

The lines – EVERY GOOD BABY DESERVES FUN

The spaces – DOGS FIGHT AND CATS EAT GOLDFISH

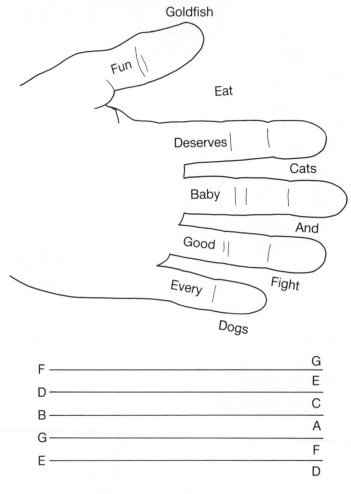

F	—————————————————	G
		E
D	—————————————————	
		C
B	—————————————————	
		A
G	—————————————————	
		F
E	—————————————————	
		D

Play this game with a friend: point to a finger or a space and your friend will tell you its letter name.

16

Leger Lines

Some notes which the violin plays are too high or too low to fit onto the stave. They are written on LEGER LINES.

Bars and Barlines

Music is written on a STAVE:

It is divided into BARS by BARLINES:

Bar   Barline

Time Signatures

The numbers at the beginning of a piece of music are called the TIME SIGNATURE. They tell you how many beats to count in each bar.

 count 4 in each bar

 count 3 in each bar

 count 2 in each bar

You will learn more about time signatures as you work through this book.

Bowing Signs

The Down Bow sign: ⊓

To play a 'down' bow, put your bow on the string and move your bowing arm *away* from your body.

The Up Bow sign: V

To play an 'up' bow, put your bow on the string and move your bowing arm *towards* your body.

Bowing Patterns

Play them every day.

 Sing, clap, and play these patterns using any notes you like.

P
Upper half

Al - to - ge - ther down up, al - to - ge - ther down up.

I like jel - ly ba - bies, I like jel - ly ba - bies.

Whole bow – upper half – whole bow – lower half

Red roof tops, red roof tops.

Lower half – whole bow – upper half – whole bow

Down up down up, stroke the bow down, up down up down, stroke the bow up.

Whole bows – varied speed

Down bow, up, down bow, up, down bow, up, down.

 Try putting several patterns together to make your own piece of music.

Repeated down bows

Down, lift, down, lift, down, lift, down, lift, stroke the bow down.

19

Basic Knowledge

1. Draw a ring around the notes which are on a line. Put a cross (X) under the notes which are in a space:

2. This note is D. Copy the note in the places marked:

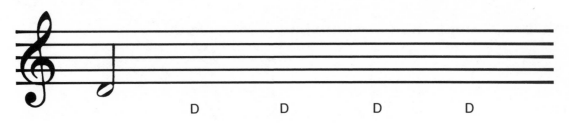

3. This note is E. Copy the note in the places marked:

4. This note is B. The stem can go up or down. Copy the note in the places marked and choose which way you would like the stem to go:

5. Practise drawing the treble clef:

20

The Open Strings

G D A E

The D string

Count: 1 2 3 4

The A string

Count: 1 2 3 4

The E string

Count: 1 2 3 4

The G string

Count: 1 2 3 4

The Crotchet

Each note receives one count.

The Minim

Each note receives two counts.

Count: 1 2 3 4

Minims on Two Strings

Is your right thumb bent?

23

The Semibreve

Each note receives four counts.

Count: 1 2 3 4

Bowing Exercises on Open Strings

24

The Semibreve Rest

Each rest receives four counts.

Count: 1 2 3 4   1 2 3 4

The Minim Rest

Each rest receives two counts.

Count: 1 2 3 4

The Crotchet Rest

Each rest receives one count.

Count: 1 2 3 4

The Rest Tests

Did you keep your wrist away from the neck of the violin?

Count: 1 2 3 4   1 2 3 4   1 2 3 4   1 2 3 4

Count: 1 2 3 4   1 2 3 4   1 2 3 4   1 2 3 4

The D String Notes

The A String Notes

A   B   C sharp   D

The First Finger on the D String

The First Finger on the A String

Elegant Aunt Bertha

Always put your fingertips on the strings.

The Second Finger on the D String

F sharp

This is the sharp sign: ♯ It makes the note one semitone higher. It lasts for the whole bar in which it is written.

P

P

P

P quick and lively

Going Shopping

P smoothly

Sea Melody

The Second Finger on the A String

C sharp

Hill and Valley March

Snakes and Frogs

I Hear Thunder

Is there enough resin on your bow?

The Third Finger on the D String

The Third Finger on the A String

Now you are ready to learn the D major scale and arpeggio on page 59.

Name the Notes (i)

Name these notes:

1.

....

2.

....

3.

....

Write these notes as semibreves:

4.

D   E   F♯   G

5.

A   B   C♯   D

Quavers

Two quavers make one crotchet beat.

Creeping Jenny

Count: 1 + 2 + 1 + 2 +

Marigolds and Daisies

Count: 1 + 2 + 3 4

I Like Caterpillars

Count: 1 2 3 + 4 +

The Dotted Minim

Each note receives three counts.

Count: 1 2 3

Note Values

1. Write the note value under each note:

....

2. Now write each bar out as a sum like this:

BAR 1	BAR 2	BAR 3	BAR 4
2			
½			
½			
1			
——	——	——	——
4			
——	——	——	——

3. Write the note value under each note:

....

4. Now write each bar out as a sum like this:

BAR 1	BAR 2	BAR 3	BAR 4
3			
——	——	——	——
3			
——	——	——	——

5. Write the note value under each note:

....

6. Now write each bar out as a sum like this:

BAR 1	BAR 2	BAR 3	BAR 4
1			
½			
½			
——	——	——	——
2			
——	——	——	——

The Slur

Count: 1 2 3 4 1 2 3 4

Count: 1 2 3 4 1 2 3 4

Count: 1 2 3 4 1 2 3 4

Count: 1 2 3 4 1 2 3 4

SM-O-O-O-O-TH B-O-O-O-O-WS

Cross strings smoothly.

Is your bow parallel to the bridge?

39

Key Signatures

The MAJOR KEY which has NO sharps at all
is called C MAJOR.

Sharp signs at the beginning of each line of music are called the KEY SIGNATURE
and show which KEY the piece of music is in.

This is F sharp. The name of the KEY is G MAJOR. The note G is the KEY NOTE.

F♯ and C♯: the KEY is D MAJOR. The KEY NOTE is D.

F♯, C♯, and G♯: the KEY is A MAJOR. The KEY NOTE is A.

REMEMBER THEM LIKE THIS!

G MAJOR	ONE SHARP	*Fish*
D MAJOR	TWO SHARPS	*Fish and Chips*
A MAJOR	THREE SHARPS	*Fish and Chips and Gravy*

Now complete the following:

1.

.....sharp

..........MAJOR

2.

.....sharp .....sharp

..........MAJOR

3.

.....sharp .....sharp .....sharp

..........MAJOR

SECTION 3

Twinkle, Twinkle Little Star

Frère Jacques

𝄞	treble clef	:‖ repeat
f	loud (forte)	*p* soft (piano)
◁	get louder	▷ get softer
pizz.	pluck the string	arco play with the bow
⊓	down bow	V up bow

Second Concert Performance

Choose a tune to play either as a SOLO – on your own; or
as an ENSEMBLE – with others.

Musical Signs

1. What do these signs mean?

f ....   *p* ....

pizz. ....   arco ....

< ....   > ....

⊓ ....   V ....

2. Fill in the meaning of the numbered signs:

(1) ....   (2) ....

(3) ....   (4) ....

3. Add signs to this tune to make it more exciting!

The G String Notes

Exercises on the G String

The Scale of G Major

Now you are ready to learn the G major scale and arpeggio on page 59.

Waltz in G

Clog Dance

andante – at a walking pace
allegro – quick and lively

> accent
⌢ pause

Can you tap the Clog Dance
rhythm with your feet?
Try dancing as you play!

MAKING UP YOUR OWN TUNE

First try out these rhythm patterns on your violin.

Now think of some different rhythms.

Clap the rhythm of your name and play it on your violin.

Now you are ready to start your tune. Try out these ideas:

1. Use the rhythms which you have played to make a tune on the open strings.

2. Choose one string and invent a tune using the notes on the string you have chosen.

3. Try inventing a tune using notes on any string you like.

4. Can you remember your tunes and play them again?

ECHO GAME

Ask your teacher or a friend to play these tunes to you. Try to play the same tune *WITHOUT LOOKING AT THE MUSIC*.

Work with a friend and play your own echo game.

Player 1
Play a very short tune.
Player 2
Try to play the same notes.

It is a good idea to agree on your starting note before you begin.

The E String Notes

E   F sharp   G sharp   A

Exercises on the E String

Now you are ready to learn the A major scale and arpeggio on page 59.

Name the Notes (ii)

1. Notes on the D string:

....

2. Notes on the A string:

....

3. Notes on the E string:

....

4. Notes on the G string:

....

Rounds

Swans on the River

Castles in the Air

Pigs in Puddles

The Fourth Finger on the E String

B

Leave a finger space between your third and fourth fingers.

0 ——— 1 ——— 2 ———— 3 ——— 4

B

The Fourth Finger Exercises

P*

1

Count: 1 2 3 4

P

2

Keep all your fingers curved on the string.

52

Little Bird

Little Bird – Ensemble Part

Moon Waltz

The tie

When a curved line connects two notes that are the same,
it is called a tie. Both notes are played in the same bow
stroke and counted as one note.

Three notes in one bow
In bar 14 three notes are connected with a slur.
Play all three notes with one up bow stroke.

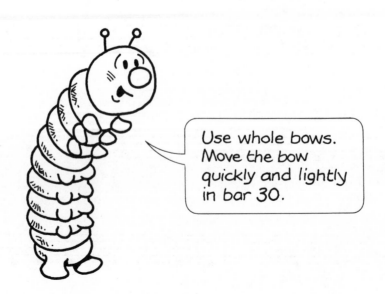

Use whole bows.
Move the bow
quickly and lightly
in bar 30.

Word Search

```
P N I L O I V X R A B P
C I F E L C E L B E R T
O P Z L R H Y T H M T Y
U R L Z V M O P T S V Q
N O M G I D C O E S Q F
T J K N O C R R H G J L
Z A I I L P A N C H Q A
E M I R A E N T T M U T
V I J T K G S B O W A O
A N O S E M I B R E V E
T O F E O L L E C U E Q
S R U L S O I S H A R P
```

Arco	*Flat*	*Quaver*	*Stave*
Bar	*Major*	*Rest*	*String*
Bow	*Minim*	*Rhythm*	*Treble Clef*
Cello	*Minor*	*Semibreve*	*Viola*
Count	*Peg*	*Sharp*	*Violin*
Crotchet	*Pizzicato*	*Slur*	

Third Concert Performance

Make up a concert programme from the music you have learned so far. You may play:

a solo;
or an ensemble with other violinists;
or an ensemble with violinists, viola players, or cellists.

Exercises to Help You Play in Tune!

LISTEN !!!
Are your fingers in
the right place ?

56

Time Signatures

This rhythm is in $\frac{4}{4}$ time. It has four crotchet beats in each bar. Clap the rhythm and count the beats:

Count: 1   2   3 + 4   1   2 + 3   4   1   2   3   4 +   1   2   3   4

This rhythm is in $\frac{3}{4}$ time. It has three crotchet beats in each bar. Clap the rhythm and count the beats:

Count: 1   2   3   1   2 + 3 +   1   2   3   1   2   3

This rhythm is in $\frac{2}{4}$ time. It has two crotchet beats in each bar. Clap the rhythm and count the beats:

Count: 1   2   1   2 +   1   2   1   2

Now write your own rhythms in the following time signatures using the note A:

1.

2.

3.

SIGHT-READING

Open string and first finger notes:

Open, first, and second finger notes:

First, second, and third finger notes:

allegro

andante

SCALES AND ARPEGGIOS

Finger Patterns for the Scales

Scales

G major

D major

A major

Arpeggios

Try playing the scales using the rhythms on page 19.

ACHIEVEMENT RECORD

Section 1

Page	√	Comment
6		
7		
9		
10		
12		
13		
13		
13		
13		
13		
13		
16		
17		
18		
19		
21		
22		
23		
24		
25		

Parts of Violin and Bow. Music Facts.

Care of the Instrument. Posture.

The Violin Strings

Open Strings Pizzicato

The Left Hand Finger Numbers

'Hopscotch'

'Hill Climbing'

'Moonlight'

'Rainbows'

'Jumping Jack'

'Fourth Finger March'

Note Learning Game

Leger Lines

Time Signatures. Bars and Barlines. Bowing Signs.

Bowing Patterns

The Open Strings

The Crotchet

The Minim

The Semibreve. Bowing Exercises on Open Strings.

Rests

First Concert Performance

solo . . . .   ensemble . . . .

date . . . .   music played . . . .

Section 2

Page	√	Comment
28		
29		
30		
32		
33		
34		
35		

The First Finger on the D String

The First Finger on the A String

Colour and Play

The Second Finger on the D String

The Second Finger on the A String

The Third Finger on the D String

The Third Finger on the A String

Page	√	Comment	
37			The Quaver. The Dotted Minim.
39			The Slur

Second Concert Performance

solo . . . .   ensemble . . . .

date . . . .   music played . . . .

Section 3

41			'Twinkle, Twinkle'
41			'Frère Jacques'
42			'Morris Tune'
42			'London Bridge'
42			'French Folk Song'
44			The G String Notes
45			Exercises on the G String
46			'Waltz in G'
46			'Clog Dance'
47			Making Up Your Own Tune
47			Echo Game
48			The E String Notes
49			Exercises on the E String
51			'Swans on the River'
51			'Castles in the Air'
51			'Pigs in Puddles'
52			The Fourth Finger on the E String
53			'Little Bird'
54			'Moon Waltz'
55			Word Search
56			Exercises to Help You Play in Tune!
58			Sight-reading
59			G Major Scale and Arpeggio
59			D Major Scale and Arpeggio
59			A Major Scale and Arpeggio

Third Concert Performance

solo . . . .   ensemble . . . .

date . . . .   music played . . . .

Comments on Posture and Style

	SECTION 1	SECTION 2	SECTION 3
LEFT HAND			
BOWING			
POSTURE			

Theory Worksheets

	√	COMMENT
WORKSHEET 1 – THE VIOLIN		
WORKSHEET 2 – THE BOW		
WORKSHEET 3 – BASIC KNOWLEDGE		
WORKSHEET 4 – NAME THE NOTES (i)		
WORKSHEET 5 – NOTE VALUES		
WORKSHEET 6 – KEY SIGNATURES		
WORKSHEET 7 – MUSICAL SIGNS		
WORKSHEET 8 – NAME THE NOTES (ii)		
WORKSHEET 9 – TIME SIGNATURES		

Overall Assessment

POSTURE AND STYLE	
SCALES	
ARPEGGIOS	
EXERCISES	
PIECES	
SIGHT-READING	
AURAL	
THEORY	
GENERAL COMMENT	

PRACTICE RECORD

Week beginning	Mon	Tues	Wed	Thurs	Fri	Sat	Sun	Parent sign here

PRACTICE RECORD

Week beginning	Mon	Tues	Wed	Thurs	Fri	Sat	Sun	Parent sign here